Love Poems

1990-2019

Yasher Koach

A G Monteverdi Press

Paperback Edition:
ISBN-13: 978-0-9600889-0-4
ISBN-10: 0-9600889-0-3

E-book Format
ISBN-13: 978-0-9600889-2-8
ISBN-10: 0-9600889-2-X

Library of Congress Control Number: 2019933304

Published by A G Monteverdi Press

DEDICATION

To my b'shert, Melissa. My beautiful twin soul; love of my life; the
final recipient of my love poems.

CONTENTS

PREFACE

This book, this compilation of poems that I have written over the course of three decades, is about love in its many forms. It is tempting to think of love poems as only being written for—or to—a subject, a recipient, that the writer desires, or has romantic, erotic feelings of love for. The Ancient Greeks had at least three words to describe the several forms of love: *philos, eros, and agape.* The first, *philos,* was a sort of brotherly love, one that a person had for one's family and siblings, even spiritual siblings. The second, *eros,* was an erotic form of love (whence comes the word, erotic), expressing romantic, sexual feelings for one of either sex. The latter, *agape,* was a complex form of love that encompassed the purest form of love, expressed for all humanity, and originated with God. The early Christians gave this term its fullest spectrum of meaning, in asserting that it represented God's love for humanity and was further embodied in a Christian's love for all of God's creations. This book contains poems that describe, circumscribe, and celebrate all these forms of love. I value these all, as expressions of the human experience; I do not discriminate. It is my hope that the reader will also value and recognize these as one reads them.

The goal of most artists is to convey their emotions, as they feel them, to the viewer-listener-witness, so that they might feel exactly and know exactly what the artist feels at the moment of conception of the art. This is likely impossible, so the artwork conveys only to a finite degree the artist's emotions and perspective. Without studying the artist's life, and even having interviews with the artist, this process is highly limited. Without a complete transfer of knowledge and sharing of identity (currently impossible in our present state of technology), full comprehension of the art thus remains impossible. And so we, as the recipient of the art tend to fill in the gaps with our own knowledge and perspective, thinking about what *we* thought when we first heard the song or read the poem, connecting it to nostalgic moments, observing it in light of what we think we know about the artist. This subjective interpretation is, at once, simultaneously valid and invalid. While the average reader may not have any knowledge of me as an author, a poet, I desire to share with you a glimpse of my world, my lived experiences; what you make of them, from your particular point of view, is now your domain. Do with them as you see fit.

In the pages that follow, I have written about my love for life, and the love *of* my life; my love for sentient beings, animals; my former loves; love for a spiritual brother; for an uncle or other family members; for all of humanity. The myriad forms of love are not confined or defined narrowly, but each such portrayal is specific to a particular moment in time and yet encompasses all love in its many forms.

I have placed these largely in chronological order of their writing, but some of them have been transposed and reinserted for thematic consistency, or in keeping with the period in my life that I am narrating. The dates are less important than how they affect the reader. I invite you to read these and enjoy them, as my offering to the muses.

Yasher Koach   Los Angeles, January, 2019.

Ode to an Ant With an Egg   April 27, 1990

Your dark little form shaking between the blades of grass
Caught my eye as it rested where you are working.
I see your precious yellow egg between your jaws
And I wonder where you mean to bring it,
Since you are so alone among the grass and weeds.
Many times I look away,
Listening to the birds singing,
And concentrate upon the hot sun shining upon my
shoulders,
And relish the faint, almost non-existent breeze cooling my
flesh.
Yet I turn back and find you still struggling amidst the dirt.
One final time, my attention is distracted.
When I return to find you,
You are gone and on your way.
I bid you a good day.

A Man in a Car   Undated (mid-2000s)

The smile of a fellow human sitting in his car, gently beaten
by the twilight sun.
Stubble covered smile, unshaven, one gold tooth shimmering
in the sunlight,
He smiles at some tune his radio shared with him.
I smile to his heart, his spirit, his humanity; he is my brother.

For Tanya, In Anticipation of the End of Spring
April 5, 1992

Had I been born a mere year before today
And had seen the seasons come and go
Only once,
Each taking its position on the world's stage
Performing their piece and retreating
Succeeded by the next,
I would assume each act to be
The season's swan song,
Never to be seen again.
You would be, to me, the Spring.
Loveliest season of them all.
I would miss you when you've gone
And wish that the year would begin again,
All over anew.
I'd wish that the Spring,
My favorite season, Lord Tennyson's 'fancy',
Would bring you back again.

Shall We?

April 4, 1992

For Tanya

Before you go,
Shall we walk amidst the oak trees of early May
And feel the smooth breeze in our hair
When the sound of gentle music comes
Wafting from established households through the air?
Before you go,
Shall we sit upon the Hill,
While newly sprouted blades of grass
Bend beneath our idle forms
And breeze has blown its course now laying still?
Before you go,
Shall we take in the view of surrounding sky
Filled with nighttime stars and crescent moon,
Shimmering in the hot and silent evening air,
Summer approaching which we cannot share?
Before you go,
Shall we take a journey over rolling hills
And walk hand in hand through rustling grass?
We'll stand before and look into each other's eyes
And savor the moment before it dies.
Before you go,
Perhaps you'll permit me a single kiss
To remember the good times when you I miss.

Neptune's Daughter   April 6, 1992

For Tanya

She appeared to me an ancient myth,
Beauty encountered in a song,
Loveliness within a dream
Like a war of prohibition and permission
I remember I struggled to meet her.
Hope was lost when she left the scene
Without bare notice or notification mean.
In middle winter she returned to
Take her place among the rich and smart
With suddenness unknown.
She resurfaced above the waves,
Fair mermaid of the deep blue oceans,
Neptune's daughter,
Enchanting lady of the open waters.
Price to pay was much too high
To get to know you,
Lost me heart and lost my mind.
--And just as suddenly. . .
. . . She was gone.
Dance among the crested waves
Tidal mountains of froth-capped doom.
Ship in a bottle to bring to your home
Take you a message from this pirate
Of New England coast, icy ports,
Who knows he'll never see you again.
Enjoy the ancient Southern seacoast,
Home of once great Seminoles

Warrior autochthons of sacred souls,
Who could not stay where they had established,
Pushed by forces greater than their own,
"Beyond their control",
To distant unknown plains strange and
Alien glades and grasses,
Reservation resting place of the remaining Indian masses.
Neptune's daughter's not too different.
Peaceful deficit of the parental pavilion
Calls you back from the lands above the waters
To breathe the bubbles beneath the waves,
In your father's realm,
Fashioned by crafty dolphins for their
Master's child upon her arrival back home.
When you sleep, darling,
Dream of me:
My ship of Northern Pirates
Who sailed beneath a Jolly Roger
Of Righteous conduct
In our attempted capture of your heart.
--And just as suddenly. . .
. . . She was gone.
Fair light angel of my unforgotten dreams
You entered when I needed you most
And fell away when your companionship meant even more.
Springtime personified,
Sea monarch's daughter,
Better than the previous best
Incomparable, without equal.
--And just as suddenly. . .
. . . She was gone.

For Tanya (Last Poem of the Era)
April 19, 1992

If I let myself fall for you, would I be a fool?
A fool dancing in the Summer wind
Upon a deep green hill
Twirling, prancing, lost in reverie
Of the gold and purple flowers he found there.
Engulfed by the beauty and wonder
Of the incredible growing life upon the hill
Beneath the brightly glowing sun
Which shines its powerful rays upon the scene.
Or would I merely be acting according to nature?
Like the Summer wind
And deep green hill
In all their splendor and glory,
Growing like they do,
Without hope or recourse,
Or even thought of an alternative path of action.

For Aimee
May 26, 1998

You said you believe your soul is young.
Because you have many confusions about the world:
"What is the nature of 'good' and 'evil?'"
"Why do bad things happen to good people?"
"What is my place in the universe?"
If your soul were old, you say,
These things would not trouble you.
My comrade, I tell you,
There is much difference 'tween experience and apathy,
Battle-hardened is not the same as jaded.
Were it so, then children would rule the world,
Because adults would no longer care.
Perhaps, Cicero was right in his description:
The dead, before they rise to life anew,
Must drink a long draught of River Lethe's waters.
Each soul must taste this hearty brew
Before a corpse we take anew.
Each one forgets its former learning,
A sin no more than the world's steady turning.
We must all attempt to recall our knowledge
To gain our degree from the cosmos' college.
These problems never go away
They merely trouble us less each learned day.
Each one of us bears Cain's penal mark,
But also each houses God's divine spark.
The sooner we remember our eternal name and true purpose
Then may our true equanimity surface.
Such is not jaded or wholly carefree;

It is simply the knowledge of a world filled with glee.
No child knows difference between right and wrong,
Though each bears an inkling of what should belong.
As each soul grows older and comes back to live,
It learns of the duties each person must give.
The purpose of each is different from another's,
And what that purpose was before.
But one thing remains the same,
The divine spark in each of us is God's holy name.
If all of the young souls were as insightful as you...
New would be old, and old would be new.
Yes, new would be old, and ancient—**brand** new!

For Krista

April 17, 2000

O, Beautiful woman, Who are you?
So soft, kind faced and open-smiled.
As I peruse your artwork hanging in the chapel,
The paintings you present are snapshots of yourself,
accepting, celebrating your ailments,
Which makes you more perfect and more real to me.
I feel a kinship for you in the expression of your infirmities,
through your art.
Imperfection at its best.
You appear to me a mystery,
Perhaps never to know in any way...
As a friend or a lover,
Or anything other than a brief acquaintance of few words,
Smiling gently, openly,
Perhaps eagerly hiding the same longings that I hold and
hide:
Longing to be free,
Longing to be happy,
Longing for you to be everything that I want you to be.
Virgin, ever-cheerful, always prudent and honorable.
Everything that I always wanted in a mate and never found,
Everything that I tried to force myself to be.
Do I long for you because you are what I do not have?
Or is it because I can truly see your soul?
Or perhaps because I do not know you and you are
So easily moldable into everything my heart desires and
knows I will never have.
Or is it simply because I am unhappy and searching for

something new?
Were I to ever have you, would you, too, turn into
A shrew, or a maniac, or a selfish brat, or any of
The others I've loved?
Like Waterhouse's *Lady of Shalot*,
Caught in time,
In the stillness of a moment,
Never growing old
Never griping, never dying.
I ask also her, will she ever reach the other side?
Will she ever climb out of her boat?
Or put her lantern down?
Were I to marry her,
Would she then flee, leaving in her place a human,
With flaws and daily chores and errands?
With weaknesses and gripes and moments of waste and fury.
I wish that you were real and yet I do not.
For if you were human you would no longer be perfect.
I love you because you are perfect, timeless, unreal.
I love you because you do not exist.

Beautiful Little Monster January 8, 2019

"Oh, my love, *mi amor*, Who held Neruda in your hand, take
me to your island",
Or something like that.
You worked on that for countless hours,
As if it were your magnum opus.
It became part of a larger paper that you never finished, but
delivered in that unfinished state,
With much excuses.
But met with the oohing, fawning approbation of sycophants.
I had to listen to it again and again as you endlessly tweaked it
and expounded upon it,
As I stood by quietly, patiently, supportive,
Like your amanuensis,
As you languished in your den of depression,
Floundering, faltering between productivity and stagnation.
I tried to encourage you, to support you, but all you could do
was weep openly and cry his name,
And explain to me that your work was not about him, but
what he represented.
He was no longer your love, but I had to smile and suppress
my anger and jealousy
Every time you worked on or recited the poem that had been
meant for him.
He, who could no longer be bothered with you.
And you won an award for your simple little poem.
So that you went to conferences and were given scholarships,
Little white girl with a Spanish name,
Oppressor of the oppressed, daughter of slave-owners

Who couldn't even roll her R's.

Lauded and applauded, as you cried and wept openly, like a performance,

And everyone was so happy to help the poor unfortunate, meek ingénue.

But the mood would change when the door would close behind you, and we would be alone,

You would expose your fangs and claws, monster that you were,

And devour my heart and my dignity.

When asked about you, later, when you were no longer in my life,

I recall saying that your soul was blacker than the Devil's heart.

That was an understatement.

Letter to Morphius, God of Dreams

December, 2000 / January, 2001

O, Morphius, why do you tease me so with dreams of my
Beloved,
With whom I cannot be?
Dreams in which we embrace a hidden, darkened embrace
As we speak of mundane things, like fixing buildings,
And so fall into each other's arms, naked,
Without a garment, even each other's fears or inhibitions,
All in the dead of night;
As we kiss a kiss of infinite passion and trust,
Fueled by a thousand years of separation,
But now undaunted by any rule, any commitment, any
woman or man.
O, cruel Morphius, why do you tease me so,
When you know these things cannot yet be?
I do so long for my Beloved and still without respite or relief,
For her cheeks reflect the sands of a thousand deserts
Which her ancestors traveled and made tame.
Her eyes recall the well by which Rachel toiled,
When Jacob beheld and loved her.
It seems only fitting that I should serve seven years to be with
her.
For even "Jacob served seven years for Rachel,
And it seemed unto him but a few days, because of the love
he had for her."
And so if I must serve seven years for her,
I will gladly do so.
But please, O Morphius, do not torment me so,

Let me be in peace while I wait.
And if I wait in vain, Morphius,
Your cruelty is inhumane.
And so, tease me no more with dreams like these,
So cruel a punishment, not even fit for Tantalus.
When long ago I held her in my arms,
In the deep of darkest night,
And we two dreamt together,
You let me dream of pleasant, hopeful things,
As I recall, you gave me visions, Morphius,
Of we two crossing bridges, hand in hand,
On adventures as soul mates, evenly yoked.
How cruel you were, Morphius, to let me dream thusly,
When you knew our love would not long last.
And now, you still torment me with visions of my Beloved.
Why can I not dream of things, like Scipio once did?
Like ancestors long gone, imparting wisdom of the soul and
outer spheres,
Something useful for my spirit, that I may know how best to
live,
In harmony with greats like Tullius and Socrates?
Or perhaps you could let me dream of prophetic things to
come,
And then interpret them,
As did Joseph for Pharaoh,
Or Daniel for his captive nation's king.
These things, of which you could let me dream, would be
useful.
But no, you still cause me to dream of my Beloved,
Who has not a sense that I even still hold a torch for her.
O, Morphius, if you cannot be helpful,
And if you know that these things can never be,

Then let me without such taunting dreams simply be.
But Morphius, if you know something that I know not,
And true such a dream may one day be,
Then perhaps a little dream of my Beloved,
From time to time,
Could not hurt too terribly much,
Just to remind me of her scent and
The feel of her touch and her embrace.

Late Night Recognitions March 8, 2001

I lie in bed
3 AM
I place another Dolmas into my mouth and finish the can.
Delicious, just like Greece.
Dead Poet's Society on the t.v.
Late night movie, not too loud.
(One of my favorites. I want to be like him, "Make your lives
extraordinary." An incredible teacher, a mentor.)
My parents asleep in the next room, asleep, in my living
room, on a makeshift bed.
Came all the way out here to take care of me after I fell ill; it
nearly killed me.
They love me. They're here to help. Just like when I was a
little kid. It's so comforting.
I'm still getting bed rest. No worries.
Nowhere to go tomorrow. No work.
I lie back and soak in the moment.
And I realize this is the greatest moment of my life.

Marcella

April 29, 2001

I met you at a bar and I kept your boyfriend lean,
As the wolves keep the caribou so.
I presented him a problem:
You were attracted to me.
I spied your voluptuous, womanly form dancing gracefully,
From across the room.
In my mind, I felt my hands upon your supple flesh,
Caressing your smooth, plump arms and shoulders,
Placing kisses upon the back of your neck,
My nose nuzzling your hair,
As I envelop you in my embrace,
Feeling your rump against my crotch
And my hands upon your full, pendulous, pointy bosom.
So, I bought you a drink even after you'd told me
You were taken.
"I have someone," you said.
I told you I thought you were very beautiful and that you
moved beautifully.
I bought you a drink just to be a good sport, I'd said.
And also to celebrate my life and my manhood.
I had escaped the jaws of death and was making the most of
it.
Had I been dead, I would never have been able
To feast my eyes upon your abundance of form.
You thanked me and we kissed each other's hands in jest and
in expression of an unfulfilled wish of passion.
We continued to make eyes at each other, from across the
room, the spoken conversation over.

And symbols of forbidden lust and desire.
He, in his corner, somewhere else, saw this,
And got jealous.
He, in his chubby, ordinary insecurity, was threatened.
You two argued outside, over cigarettes,
A few hugs and some gesticulations—each vying for
dominance.
You still sneaked a few stolen lustful glances with me.
You disappeared.
I left.
I'd made your day,
Making you feel beautiful and special.
I kept him lean, like the wolf and the caribou,
And told him,
Without words,
To appreciate you,
Or I might be back.

Weird

May 19, 2001

I know that I am ugly, unattractive,
Stupid looking and weird.
I've been told as much.
I understand that no woman would ever look at me with
desire,
Except the ugly ones, unattractive, unfit—like me.
I am too intellectual, too deep, too intense,
Too nerdy, too needy, too clingy, too loving, too wanting,
Too immature, too poor, too ordinary, too common,
Too educated, too short, too skinny, too fat, too weak,
Too uncool, too different, too strange.
No one would ever see anything in me worth looking at
twice.
I was lucky to ever have a girlfriend, even the bad and abusive
ones.
No one likes the car I drive, the place I live in,
The length of my hair, the size of my nose, the size of my
member.
I'm not cool enough;
I can't dance well, or really at all, except moshing;
But who does that anymore, except misfits like me?
Trying too hard, trying to be different, trying to be free,
Trying to be confident, trying to be the center of attention,
That's what *she* said. Trying to be funny; trying just too hard.
Trying to be Me.
What about you?
Do you really have the right to judge me?
Were you there through all that I've been through?

All that made me what I am, are you any different?
Are you anything but a child trapped in an adult's body?
Unsure, unsafe, insecure, yearning to be loved, comforted,
Reassured, listened-to, heard, understood, desired.
I understand you. I comprehend you.
I have compassion, sympathy for you.
That is what makes me wonderful,
More than Human: that I feel for you.
I have survived the jaws of Death,
I comprehend.

For Skolie   May 19, 2001

He sits there in the bar,
Day after day, night after night.
Waiting for someone to arrive to save him,
Set him free.
Someone to love him, need him, understand and accept him.
Sometimes he starts fights or causes trouble,
Sometimes he comments inappropriately.
But most often he just sits—lonely—facing the bar,
A phalanx of draughts each harder than the next,
Or stares into the jukebox, trying to find the perfect song
which will
Give expression to the pain in his heart,
Tell the world of what he needs.
He has friends, but he feels alone.
I'm kind to him, despite his initial unwelcoming words,
But he knows I care.
He can see it in my eyes,
That my soul yearns to make him my brother
And show him that it's all going to be okay.

In Memoriam   May, 2001

I installed a small monument today beside a lonely sapling of
a tree.
It was placed there by your father in honor of thee,
And read your name and the span of your life: Mark Locher
1956-1994
You had lived a short life, and uneventful by my account.
I'd known your father, briefly,
But never knew that he'd even had a son.
Through heavy rock and tight-clenched dirt, we'd broke,
To sink the pole with a plaque bearing your name.
In this task I'd gotten the opportunity to honor you and to
know you,
Though we'd never met, or said a word.
I honor thee who has gone to live with the majority.
But the question still remains for me,
How shall we remember thee?
What did you do that we should remember you?
Who were you, and what did you do?
Did you save the Athenians from certain Spartan death?
Or follow the ranks of Ulysses or Achilles?
Or follow Caesar as he crossed the Rubicon?
Had you freed a people enslaved?
Or led a young nation to victory in independence?
Had you done anything noteworthy for which to be
remembered,
In your short life, hardly any older than I?
Evidently one man thought you had.
The impression you made upon him was your legacy,

The love and loyalty you'd given to a father who thought the
world of you,
That he would erect a monument for all the world to see,
Moreso to brag that he had had a son, such as thee.

Roma   July 12, 2001

I saw you enter the Roman café at the university, your long,
wavy raven hair accenting your olive skin.
Your eyes, framed by arcs of fine hair on your brow, the
strokes of an artist's brush.
Your lips, full but pouting over nothing,
You were reserved and aloof and I wanted to touch you and
gain your favor,
But you were elsewhere, lost in thought, perhaps pondering
Pompeii or Herculaneum.
I saw reflected in your eyes the Tiber and the waters of Trevi,
Your figure was slender and lithe, womanly yet sparing.
Your full breasts, heavy laden as with milk, were the bosom
of the hills of Rome.
Thy two breasts are the same which suckled Romulus and
Remus,
When you were in the form of a she-wolf, now infinitely
more beautiful as a woman.
My friend and I watched you, enthralled, unable to look away
from your unearthly beauty.
But you were undisturbed as you sipped your milky-tan
colored tea from a clear glass bowl-shaped cup,
Holding the pierced handle with two fingers,
And ate your cookies in silence,
And left, without ever looking at another human being.
You were to me the most beautiful woman of Rome.
You were, in fact, Rome, herself.
My Roma, nameless woman, *bella donna* sent by Venus to
grace us for the present moment,

Only to fade into memory of this trip which made me fall in love with your city, ever wishing to return.
You who rivaled Pygmalion's creation, Galatea, in beauty among women.
Sent by Neptune's daughter in her stead,
You were the womb that bore Aeneas' race and the hips that carried his nation.
I will love you always, longing for your touch and to know your human name.

Equine Tympani
July 21, 2001

In the night I longed for you and felt as if I'd burst.
I desired with all my force of being to hold you and draw you
near,
But you were far away and I could not reach you.
I knew that I must invoke my patron, Seneca,
To free myself from bonds that fettered me.
That in my continence I might endeavor to undertake
something great, as did he or his own patron Socrates,
Overcoming weakness and fear,
Taming the passions with reason
That they may survive Death.

I awoke in the middle of the night, my heart screaming,
Pounding like the hooves of a herd of horses,
Equine Tympani.
I could not let go of the though of your hand in mine,
Your body in my arms,
Your tongue and breath in my mouth.
I breathed your essence as air,
Your love—unrequited.

Eros' Darts   Summer, 2001

Hidden love, centuries old it seems,
Unspoken, secret words and passions I've never felt for
another.
Cramped and crammed into one heart, unable to be exposed,
Unfair.
Whatever shall I do?
I'm lying to myself and to my best friend.

To sneak a glimpse of my Sheba as she sleeps
Separated from me, it seems, by a thousand miles,
In separate beds.
She sleeps in beauty as did Eros when Psyche did sneak her
fatal glimpse of him.
I have watched her sleep before.
As on the train five years hence,
When she rested her head innocently, carefree, on my
shoulder
And I dared not move or touch her for fear
That I'd wake her and disturb the perfect image.
I have been bitten by Eros' passion-poison-tipped darts.
Held in paralysis so that I cannot move or change.
Dreadfully discouraged, I am not permitted to touch her as I
would.
But I watch her as she sleeps, she not knowing my love for
her, my hidden desire.
She is my soul mate, but she does not know.
She is my one desire, but she does not know.
I am helpless, crippled, manacled,

For fear that my words will destroy our simple bonds of
friendship,
Scare her away like a wild deer that has come to drink from a
stream, accosted by a predator.
She is to me that doe and I the hunger.
But I have no arrows.
I merely watch;
I await Eros to lend me his.

I Laugh

September 3, 2001

I see the wrinkles slowly climbing onto my face,
And vaguely remembering the process as if
From lifetimes before.
Many processes like this leave me feeling
As if I cannot remember what it was like
Before each change.
But this time, I am conscious
At the moment of conception.
I see the gestation of the wrinkle begin.
I don't like it and long for yesterday's
Clear face,
Angry at this process, having almost convinced myself that it
would never start;
That I might be the one to avoid the next step.
Angry that I too must grow old.
Yes, I begin to remember the process from before,
Some other lifetime; some other body.
And the irony strikes me that I am
Lamenting one step in an eternally cyclical process.
I've been young before and will be young again.
I laugh.
And I laugh heartily,
Like a man who survived the Jaws of Death by meningitis.
That, I am,
I laugh and remember that
My laugh is still young.
It has not changed or withered,
Spoiled or wrinkled.

In fact it has become young again.
Reborn.
New.

The Press   September 29, 2001

For Lisa

I met you at a bar;
You were the singer.
Your long red hair,
Auburn – dyed, I think – framing a pretty face,
Honest, wholesome, almost angelic, reminiscent of my cousin
Lucy's,
Hippy-ish, gentle, comforting, framed by rectangular,
Black-rimmed nostalgi-glasses.
You sung with the voice of an angel, playing guitar.
Instantly, I knew you.
We smiled, our gazes met.
Immediately I was transported into a world in the future, one
of possibilities,
Where you were my wife.
There you were, standing in the kitchen, making tea,
Coming back to bed on a Sunday morning,
Rainy, bleak, illumined only by your gentle honest face,
Peering at me from my embrace.
I saw you cooking earthy foods, with spices I'd never heard
of,
For friends we called ours – not mine or yours.
I saw you discussing with me your change of jobs or
promotion,
Encouraging mine.
I saw you holding our child – one, two, or three?
I saw you growing old gracefully with me
In a two story house, not a cabin, but rustic, old-fashioned,

Near my college where I'm a professor.
You encouraged me, stood beside me, accompanied me.
This is what I saw as you stood there
Singing, strumming your guitar.
Chords I don't know with my hands, but know with my ears.
Am I wrong or right?
Is it you, or just a whim?
Because when I look at you, I see Forever.

Nameless Love October 17, 2001

I have to write this; it's burning in my heart.
I love you, but I don't know your name.
I thought I knew it, two, three, maybe four times…
But I was wrong.
I've always loved you and never knew your name.
I could feel your soul,
Know the taste in your mouth,
The scent of your skin,
The pressure of your touch,
The sound of your laugh,
Feel your cheek next to mine,
Even know your thoughts.
But I don't know your name,
Or even if you really exist.
But you have to; You're so real to me.
I see it in other couples now and then;
I know the feeling.
I know we would have that
If I ever found you.
But I don't even know if you're real.
I know you and you are my best friend.
I can feel the rapport and connection.
But who are you?
I know that you long for me in your own heart.

Parking Lot Showcase   November 2, 2001

I sit in my car on a sunny day, biding time, outside the auto-
parts store.
And watch them cavort, associate, convivialize.
Three or four chunky Latin chicks baring themselves
For the pleasure of the world, the male gaze.
Showing arms, legs, shoulders, bellies,
But nothing more, for fear the Pope will see and disapprove.
Show me your plump flesh, tinted by the sun,
Different shades of tan and yellow or bronze,
Fed plump by corn and rice.
You attract and advertise for bald-shaven men
To fuck you and beat you or neglect you.
It's all you know, so that you'll have someone to love you
unconditionally,
A baby new and clean.
Shamefully, these men know no better.
They are just as afraid and alone as you,
Trained for indifference and ignorance,
But better trained at hiding it within their machismo.
I desire you, but I will not touch you,
For I pity you, and I fear you,
That by loving you, I become wrapped up in your world of
pain, your drama,
And unbroken cycle of abuse.
I will not take part.
But I admonish your men:
Respect and cherish these, for these are the source of life.

Galatea, Helen   November 15, 2001

I still find your long red hairs lingering on my floor and on
my pillow.
Perhaps if I find enough of them, I might recreate you,
A version of you all my very own.
As Pygmalion did Galatea, and in her have his very own
Venus.
Shall I,
To have a version of you all to myself?
Thirty years to find you and now I must share you?
Come away with me Helen, and leave your Menelaos—your
two children.
Oh, would that I might have you all my own.
To play and frolic in the sun and rain,
As you could not do in your first attempt at love,
As I have never done, waiting for you.
And now I fear that I may never have you.
I cannot expect you to leave your world,
The realm where you are queen without a king.
And I cannot leave mine to be your king.
But maybe one day, when they are grown,
We may ally our realms to form a kingdom all our own.

Nap Date

You and I should buy a bed
Just for you and me,
Brand new, with no memories or fears or connections,
And place it in the middle of the yard,
Where no one will ever suspect a thing,
Because we've nothing to hide and are hiding nothing.
And when we're tired, we can sleep:
Sleep a sleep of a thousand days and a thousand nights,
To make up for the time we've spent apart,
And lie in each other's arms,
Awake-asleep-awake again,
Flirting with sleep, first you, then me.
And I can watch you as you dream,
A gentle smile on your pretty lips that seem to me
Like they are always ready to crack a smile.
I would like for you to sleep,
Held tightly in my arms, protected, happy,
Feeling warm, safe, treasured, loved, respected.
And I can caress your cheeks and forehead
With my fingertips and lips
And watch you dream a dream
Of me holding you in my arms as you dream
(A dream within a dream).
And if I drift, I may awake,
And catch you, watching me
In a dream of you watching me as I sleep,
(Another dream within a dream)
With you in my arms (girl of my dreams),

Looking up at me with your pretty eyes ablaze with contentment.

The Press Revisited

February 9, 2002

When I entered the bar, and met you,
I had nothing to lose, I was confident.
I flirted with you as if I were Julius Caesar,
Confident enough to cross the Rubicon.
Now there is so much to lose,
I am timid and afraid to lose your love and respect.
Any wrong turn, any misstep.

To tame the Ukrainian lioness….
How can you take the lion from the jungle?
To place her in a cage would be cruel and inhumane,
No matter how well-gilded.

To drink of the nectar of your mouth,
Whence comes angels' voices that I hear when you sing.
How I long to hear that voice tell me that it loves me.
How I long to write poetry for you in the evenings
And have you sing me songs you've written for me.
To sit on a swing on our porch and cuddle, dreaming of
nothing.
Will I ever hold your attention completely?
Will I ever have your total devotion?
If I offered you my hand, would you take it?
Or just hold it for a minute and let it go?
I want to be your partner and your lover,
Your best friend and sibling in the Lord,
But never your keeper or tamer.
I would rather let you go if I would never

Hold your heart in my hands
To kiss and caress in exchange for my own.

Those Eyes

February 11-14, 2002

For Lisa

Girl of my dreams, I think that you are,
When we had our first date,
You removed your glasses and I caught a glimpse
Of your eyes, piercing blue-green,
Passionate yet holy, like some mystical creature,
Or some sorceress who can cast spells and
Charm men with one glance of her gaze.
That must be why you wear glasses,
So as not to have a line of men following you,
And thereby to conceal your powers until needed.
When you removed those glasses, revealing your secret
powers,
You must have intended to use them on me;
You charmed me and I have never been the same.
Each time you look at me and our eyes meet,
I am under your spell; in your power, glasses on or off.
When we sat at the bar five nights hence, you cleaning your
lenses,
Once again, I caught a glimpse – lion's shining eyes,
As if reflecting glints of moonlight in the silent, lightless
Serengeti.
The night you slept in my bed, when I awoke and you stirred.
Those eyes gazing back at me, I was yours.
Even the surreptitious embrace that you 'foisted' upon me
well before dawn,
Was simply enough to enslave me, even with your eyes
hidden by the darkness.

Time and time again, you cast your spell upon me and
I am yours. I have no choice but to simply be such.
And I long to gaze into those eyes.
The spell has overtaken me like a sweet and subtle poison
Insinuating deeper into my heart.
Having been bitten deeply or stung and injected with a potion
Or elixir that has charmed and enthralled me.
Like an addiction to some strange, unnamed drug,
That I might call Lisa.
When I think about your kiss, my mouth waters for this drug
called "Oath of God."
I long to taste the nectar of your mouth,
Whence come angels' voices that I hear when you sing,
As if a siren, like those that taunted Ulysses and his crew
nearly to watery grave.
I long to hear that voice and see those eyes
That have enthralled and entranced me.
We are too often divided,
Separated by too many miles.
Like the two lovers from antiquity,
As they were divided by a wall,
And were forced to swear their love through a hole therein,
Perhaps I could catch a glimpse of those eyes that enthrall me
While conversing through that hole.
But would that we would meet a gentler end than those two,
Both dead from haste and misunderstanding,
Confused by a bloodied veil, dropped in flight from a hungry
lion.

I am confident that you will use your powers for good,
heavenly agent that you are,
Oath of God, Elishevah,

I want to run against the breeze with you,
The wind in our faces.
I want to paint a house with you,
Classic with gingerbread trim and old porcelain fixtures
And red brick fireplaces.
Will you let me care for you?...
Will you let yourself care for me
With the passion and intensity of ten thousand suns,
And the constancy of the tide which never ceases
To lap against the shore, kissing it and caressing it,
As I cannot help but do to your cheeks when under the spell
of your eyes and voice.

Frightened children we are,
Searching for a home.
I offer you my heart and my embrace as a home,
If you wish,
If you'll offer me the same –
A place of prime real estate in your heart, nestled in your
bosom,
Wrapped tightly in your truest embrace.

Precarious   March 9, 2002

The occasional pain of a dream about a lost love,
Unrelenting, unrequited, persisting,
Is not too much to bear.
But it lingers and reminds, giving dull ache gradually subsiding
Never to return.
The pain I feel of an aborted love,
Unfulfilled, unconsummated, incomplete,
Plagues me every morning, every night
Like a monster in the shadows,
Waiting for a moment of weakness,
Dropping my shield, letting my unconscious go to work.
I suffer for her: *Ponesa* (I suffer).
Having had to excise her for excessive affronts,
I am in great pain,
Feeling betrayed, sickened, abandoned.
As the day wears on,
The pain subsides, hiding behind walls, peering out over window sills,
Watching me, waiting to determine a good moment to attack.
Will you ever open your heart to someone completely,
And leave it that way, my Fair One?
Or will you always hold it out for me to stroke and caress,
And then retract it in fear,
Chanting, "I'm fine. Nothing's wrong. I'm strong. I need nobody."
Like a child whistling in the darkness to allay her fears.
Your "survival mode" is like that of a child, frightened

By the blindfold placed on her for the piñata game.
She bats blindly at anything in her vicinity,
Much less to get the goodies than to beat the "baddies",
Angry at her loss of sight,
Made fearful by stupid rules and adults that ignore
Her fear of the dark.
She feels empowered by the stick
And uses it against everyone around her,
Hurting even those she loves.
Our love is precarious, teetering on a dangerous edge,
Insecure, unsafe to leave unattended.
And so I must excise her from my life and my heart
Before I am hurt by her wild batting.
My love for her plagues me daily,
But I will not abide in being pushed—or batted—away.

Perfect

Once or twice you've tried to remind me
That you are not perfect.
What is perfect?
The way you sat in my car and picked at your teeth with a
toothpick, as ladylike as you could muster, embarrassed to let
me see you?
That was perfect.
When I heard you blow your nose for the first time and it
sounded somewhere between a 'Bronx Cheer' and an airplane
taking off, the way my grandfather used to blow his nose.
That was perfect.
The way you say "pitcher" instead of "picture".
That is perfect.
The way your butt looks in tight jeans.
That's perfect.
The way you got dirt under your finger nails the first weekend
you were packing to move and you were embarrassed about
how they looked.
That was perfect.
The way that a few of your silvering roots show through
beneath your shock of beautiful red hair, symbolizing the
strength gained from many years of heartache and loneliness
staved off by faith and optimism.
That's perfect.
The way that little tan beauty mark sits just within sight on
your right breast, when you wear something revealing.
That's perfect.
The way your hands feel in mine when we skip across the

street together – like that of my best friend.
That's perfect.
The way you surprise me every now and then and playfully
bite my neck, making me so aroused and passionate that it
tests the huge reserves of willpower that God gave me to help
preserve my chastity until more appropriate times.
Shame on you. But that's perfect.
The way you 'nimbly' spilled and splattered your tea on
Valentine's Day and feared that I'd be angry, eventually
realizing I wasn't and was just grateful to have you in my life
and my arms.
That's perfect.
The way you playfully told me in vague terms that I should
never worry about being embarrassed or spurned by your
answer if I asked you to marry me, effectively giving me the
go-ahead.
That's perfect.

These are the things that make me want to marry you
And hold you tightly in my arms for the rest of my days.
The things that make you perfect –
Perfect for me.

Idyllic

March 20, April 3, April 27, 2002

I want our life to be idyllic,
Everything we've worked so hard for.
Our life and love a celestial reward, given from above,
Prayers answered, like a dream come true.

Once or twice you've asked if you can get me
Anything, a drink or snack, from in the kitchen,
"You just sit and relax there, Love,
What men in this family do;
Ask for what you'd like me to bring,
And I'll bring it right to you."
All I ask of you is this, Love:
Bring me a sample of your finest kisses,
And a serving of your deepest love.
I have need of nothing else.

And in return, these things can I offer:
Toilet seats left down – lid, too;
Toothpaste tubes, squeezed from the bottom
(Caps screwed on in place);
Dirty socks placed in the hamper;
Garbage taken out at night;
Eternal fidelity, not one slip;
(And I'll really believe that you're the most beautiful woman
in the world;
Never will I wish you were another.);
Phone calls every night if I'm away,
Just to tell you that I miss you and to hear about your day.

When you cry, I want for you to turn to me and never turn
my love away.
When I cry at "South Pacific",
I don't want to cry alone anymore.
I want to cry while holding you in my arms,
Kissing your red hair, that covers your sweet face,
With eyes that have already closed,
Fast asleep, because you've watched this movie
With me a million times already,
And you've seen me cry a million and twelve.
No more playing the role of Joe Cable,
Dying for his country, leaving his true love
On an island, all alone,
Bali Hai,
But having accepted the part of Emile DeBecque,
Returning to his own "Cock-eyed Optimist",
Whom he met singing in a bar
So long ago,
With her black glasses shielding hypnotic, magical,
Sorceress' eyes that gleamed at him,
Smiling, waiting for the set break to arrive,
So that she could strike up a conversation
With the man of her dreams,
The man she would one day marry.
Sweet *Elishevah*, 'Oath of God',
Come out of the castle, replete with moat and drawbridge,
That you built so long ago.
Slip out of your "something sexy - satin, steel, armor tight"
That you donned so long ago.
I will not make you cry, but would dry your tears
And take you as my partner through my life,

As my true love, as my wife.

Let me slip into your heart, like a sweet and subtle poison,
An elixir draught, not bad but good,
That insinuates and permeates your soul (or spirit)
With all my deepest, and truest, love.
Let my love wash over you like the waves of the shore,
Let my love surround and warm and comfort you,
Let it bathe you like rays of sunlight resting on the sand.
Let me love you,
Let your heart seek mine.

Little Girl Lost

May 17, 2002

When will I ever fully know you,
And fully own your heart?
Once upon a time, I thought I knew you,
And thought I held your heart.
The night I held your hand and couldn't let go,
And desperately wanted to kiss you but thought I should not,
Our first date.
The night I lay next to you and you held me close in your
arms,
And I awoke, morning calm gazing at your still dreaming
face.
So long ago, as memories stretched paper thin.
(Thinner than gossamer memories spoken of by a former
lioness)
We were closer then, than we are now,
And we grow more distant by the day,
Every moment that you push me away,
Every day that you are afraid to seek my love
And I afraid to call and face your cold and heartless embrace.
You are a little girl lost.
Haunted by the face of every man you loved,
That ever pierced your heart with poison tipped arrows.
No wonder that you fear the elixir of my love,
That insinuates like a poison ever deeper into your heart;
You fear it will maim and kill rather than heal.
But your fear may poison our love,
Starving our spirits to the point where we will no longer
hunger

For each other's kiss or sustenance,
But, like starving children that grow indifferent to the
Feeling of an empty belly, no longer caring for food,
Grown comfortable with its empty warmth,
We run the risk of dying without ever truly knowing
The feeling of true love and the sustenance it can bring us
If we accept God's gift brought into our lives.
I am not to be feared.
Fear me not,
Burt fear the thought of being without me,
Having spurned God's gift of our love,
And driving me away as if a wolf or wild dog.
Fear the thought of losing my love,
Turned away in a wasteful, selfish, self-destructive moment,
More to be feared than the fears you hold dear.
I intend to be in this life, your greatest ally,
Your truest love, your closest friend.
All I've ever wanted was to love you,
And be your partner, your confidant, your lover, husband and
mate.
The one you cry to, the one you laugh with,
The one you turn to first.
And after all this, still, I ask,
Let my love wash over you like the frothing tide,
Sipping at the shore, baked slowly by the sun.
And I will ask you again, like a request of betrothal,
Until you either let me in or drive me away.
But I no longer accept your empty half-steps,
Followed by dreadful fear, masked by denial of facts,
Languishing in frightful terrors of what it means to be
vulnerable to me.
"Oath of God", my poetry is not merely pretty words, devoid

of meaning,
Composed to woo or court you.
But accept these as oaths of my own, in God,
Each word, each phrase a vow,
A kiss, a promise.

Requiem for a Dead Uncle

October 13, 2002

I weep for you, Uncle.
On your death bed,
Many times revived.
Stuck with tubes and strapped,
"Do not resuscitate," the proxy order said,
Signed finally by your loving wife,
Who had wished you dead many times in your marriage.
I'm sorry that you had such a tough life,
Fraught with failure caused by fear of success.
Ralph Cramden, ever driving your bus,
Failed businesses, Big Man on Campus who never made it
big;
Your nightclubs where you slept,
Watching the profits disappear, embezzled by thieving
colleagues;
With your horse racing, your Pick sheets and your systems,
A failproof scheme, a sure bet.
It ended, too.
Little boy that grew up too fast
Because of what he saw.
Whose thighs were touched by unwanted hands,
Whose eyes saw things a little boy should never see
Even in nightmares.
Who saw his baby sister raped and tortured by those
Trusted to be near.
Whose grandfather beat and ravished her unspeakably
And made you watch,

With your eyes, with your eyes.
What you saw with your eyes.
I weep for you, poor man,
Who dies.

Requiem for a Dead Cat   July 31, 2011

For "Sammy"

When my wife saw you in the road, you were still alive,
barely.
Your head popped up, turned, moved.
She called me; asked what to do.
Nearby, I prepared a towel, some gloves, and some phone
numbers.
I hopped in and we sped back to see you,
If you were still alive.
I don't know whether thankfully or not,
But you had been hit again, once? Twice?
Mercy.
One quick dash to the head, and you were dead,
Your little skull crushed,
Your right eye, emerged, bloodshot, sightless.
The rest of you, still warm,
Still limp when I picked you up with gloved hands,
As if you were to wake up, in just a moment.
Someone loved you, I should think.
Or if not, then someone should have.
No tags, no signs of grooming.
Kitty-cats don't just come from thin air.
Someone is responsible for each.
Shame on them.
Shame on every driver for not stopping.
Shame upon each one that hit you and didn't stop.
A curse upon each of them, that they should suffer what you
suffered.

What we did, to pick you up and bring you to your ultimate
rest,
I know it didn't help stop your suffering, or save your life,
But it seemed the right thing to do.
When we dropped you off,
And the nighttime workers let us in,
It felt so inhumane, so sterile,
So impersonal, to drop your body off wrapped in a plastic
bag or two.
Asked to pay the $25 dollar fee, I scoffed, saying,
"It wasn't our animal."
That made me feel guilty that I wasn't willing to pay your
Charon's fare,
But it seemed an insult to ask us, the do-gooders, to pay a fee.
We left your body on the counter, unceremoniously,
As if there should have been more,
A funeral, some mourning.
You were alive, once.
And then you weren't.
I wish I had met you and could pet you,
While you still lived.
I'm sorry.
I'm sorry that you died.
I'm sorry that there was no one there to comfort you when
you died.
We did what we could.

Ravenhair

June 7, 2003

For Penelope

I remember the feeling of your raven hair brushing on my
forehead and cheeks like black feathers.
I remember your lips brushing against mine.
I remember your tongue in my ear, and how I'd never felt
anything so exquisite before.
I remember my pelvic mound against yours as we moved
together in frottage.
I remember your scent.
I remember the sound of your breathing as you slept in my
arms.
I remember your eyebrows, full and deep.
I remember your full breasts heaving upon my chest as you
lay atop me and we kissed, playfully, probative.
I remember the gold chain that hung between them, with a
pendant of a *chai*.
I recently found a note left by one lover for another in front
of a house near our *alma mater*, as people cleared out and
prepared to leave the lives they had known there for an
instant.
It read, "Chris, I love you desperately; I love you madly."
I wished in that moment that I had said that to you before we
parted.

Is There More Than This?   April 25, 2004

Darius, My Brother:
You once told me that you scan the stars and
You sometimes wonder if there is more than this.
I tell you what I see.
There is nothing more than this:
To make a difference, to make our mark,
To touch as many lives as we can,
To do good and to teach impressionable young minds
How not to be so impressionable;
And to be remembered
By our peers,
By our lessers,
By our descendants - biological or spiritual.
To rise above the noise and hype,
To live as the ancient sages and
Philosophers have taught us to live,
With bravery in the face of death - and life equally so -
With great gusto
And passion for life,
Living simply and virtuously
Within the framework that the Gods
And our ancestors have laid for us.
It is ours to honor those who made us,
Our ancestors and their Gods alike
And to teach future generations respect -
Be they by our flesh or by our spirit.
You have done all this, my Brother,
And all you need to do -

All there is for us -
Is to continue to do this.
Be content with this Darius,
And you will be among the ranks
Of our greatest ancestors,
The wisest and most noble of men and women,
And you will never want for anything
And your name will live forever,
Namesake of the Great King of Persia,
Whose name means 'bringer of the good'.
Be brave, Darius,
Accept your greatness,
And do well,
Bring the good.

The Earrings   May 11, 2004

For Melissa

Last night you left your earrings behind,
And went back home to clear your mind.

I tried to cuddle with your sweet earrings,
But they were sharp and not much use to me.

Your lovely form was soft and warm,
And indeed much better company.

Next time, please stay and fill my bed,
And send your earrings home instead.

You Ask Me Why　　　May 23, 2004

For Melissa

You ask me why I love you so intensely after only a short
while.
With all due care and respect, My Love, the question is
absurd.
Who among us will ask a young mother why she instantly
loves her newborn child?
Or why the ocean loves the shore and laps gently at it higher
and higher with the tide,
Gradually receding to let the seashore rest, but ever returning
to its mate?
Or why the plants and trees love the sunlight and will bend
and stretch to greet it.
Why the sun and moon love the sky, seeking endlessly to rise
to its peak,
And even when tired, retiring to the depths of the earth,
They rise yet again to greet and kiss her.
Why music loves the dance?
Leads many to rise up to rhythmic motion and express their
passions,
As does my own True Love.
My answer is that it is natural for some things to love one
another.
Fate brings them together and it's often unwise to question
why.

Cabin in the Woods   June 5, 2004

For Melissa

Bury me deep inside your love.
And never let me go,
Join me in a cabin in the woods of the universe.
Grow old—or young—with me…whichever.
Coat your fingers in delicate spices of lovely cooking,
Dishes planned in a moment's notice and of your love.
Moments of unconscious, unplanned bliss
Miles away from the nearest gremlin,
Far from the voices of our past
That used to call to us and
Prevent forward progress,
Dragging us back into fear and self-doubt
And doubt of each other's love.
These moments of organic bliss (in every sense organic)
Will have caught us unawares
In that cabin in the woods
Of the universe (or university)
Taking our refuge, building our home,
Ages of games of love;
Whipped cream, chocolate, lingerie, costumes, belly-dancers
and Romans,
Sweat, juices flowing, passion ignited again and again.
Memories created, cherished, reworked and constantly
renewed.
Cooked in the juices of our love,
With those exotic spices from our hippie garden
Behind our little cabin in the woods of the university.

Be my little Dharma; I'll be your little Greg,
A little bit of each in the other—
Ideal couple of the century or maybe longer.
Let's fulfill our dreams together,
In RVs and on Greyhounds,
In tiny cars or big, boat-like ones.
Having all come to look for America and the university.
Flat tires no problem,
Each event an adventure,
Far beyond our wildest dreams.
Each day a brand new live
Because variety's the spice of life,
Variety within constancy is the key to longevity.
I'll teach and preach to the world,
You can dance and heal and teach as well,
Incomparable couple we'll be,
In our cabin in the woods of the university.

Promises   June 25, 2004

Scared to accept, scared to receive.
I'd forgotten how to love
In a way that would bring someone closer than arms' length.
It's one thing to love the world and close the door to my cell
When the homeless go home,
And the soup kitchen is closed.
It's another to find you there
Waiting for me in my room
In my bed, when the day is over
And the day's good deeds are done.
To have you close to me
Was hard, but well worth the shock of change.
Don't ever let my hand go free.
Don't ever let this miracle change.
Kisses before breakfast and half past three.
Love notes on the car seat and under the pillow.
CDs in the morning mail.
Kisses after midnight and well before dawn.
Promise that we will ever grow closer,
The draw of mystery replaced with intimacy.
Comfort.
Stability
The absence of fear
Or threat of loss.
That with every kiss and embrace
We grow closer
Fulfilling our destiny,
Completing our bond.

Something Missing June 27, 2004

This morning I awoke with a profound sense of something
missing;
Not lacking, gone, or even less, awry,
But as if something were misplaced.
In a moment, I knew that what was missing -
Was you,
Still in my life,
Still within my love (and I in yours),
But not in bed beside me.
There was no great pain,
As if I'd lost,
But a dull ache,
Knowing that you were elsewhere and I here.
We are, my love has said, "Beautiful Twin Souls"
And when we are apart
We are no less so,
But like two magnets,
Desiring to be placed together,
Pulling, yearning to be with their mate,
Even stronger when together!

For a Belly Dancer October 21, 2004

O Faithful goddess,
Whose hips are like rolling hills,
Whose movement is like the ocean—
Swelling, rising, falling, undulating, calling, beckoning.
Whose belly, like a gentle mound
Would make the kings of old desire to be entombed in.
Who would make the Minoan snake goddess writhe with
envy,
Whose dance would make the Terpsichorean Muse question
who is the artist and who the muse.
Full-figured Indian goddess,
Who resembling ideals from ancient past
Might teach men and women of today
What truly is beauty.
You are the embodiment of all that is truly feminine,
The supple strength of your thighs and bottom,
The smoothness of your alabaster skin.
The flaring breadth of your hips.
The fullness of your arms.
The swell of your supple belly.
The perfection of your ample bosom.
Your sweet, angelic face with the warmth of your welcoming,
comforting smile.
All echoing your nurturing, nourishing nature,
Protective of your brood,
Ready to defend with the fangs of Kali,
What is flesh of your flesh.
I revere, honor, and worship you for all my days.

ABOUT THE AUTHOR

Yasher Koach is an academic scholar by profession. He lives in Los Angeles with his beloved wife, where he pursues his word craft as a passionate avocation to be fulfilled within the confines of a life lived for all humanity, and as ancillary to the trade that feeds his family. This is his second book, but his first book of poetry, and the first to be published under the present *nom de plume*.

YASHER KOACH